Today *is a* New Day *Tomorrow is Too!*

Your Path to Weekly Motivation & Inspiration

GERI A. CONDON

Today is a New Day—Tomorrow is Too!
Your Path to Weekly Motivation and Inspiration

ISBN 9781645382454
First Edition

Today is a New Day—Tomorrow is Too!
Your Path to Weekly Motivation and Inspiration by Geri A. Condon

For information, please contact:

ten16press.com
Waukesha, WI

Editor: Lauren Blue
Cover & Interior Design: Kaeley Dunteman

This book is dedicated to all those who recognize the importance of acknowledging mental health. Also, to my Grandma Orler, who died too soon, but left me with the sense for loving all and the importance of service to others.

Table of Contents

In Gratitude

One of my biggest blessings has always been my friends, my cheerleaders, my tribe! In this book endeavor, they have not failed me. My tribe is comprised of women across the country. They have known me from as far back as kindergarten to high school, college, my original government profession to my current mental health profession, and from thirty years of living in McHenry, Illinois. My dear friend, Dorothy Wolf, who always jumps in to support me in any and every way and is my "go-to," was the first to glimpse and review my dream in this book. I trust her honesty and gentle criticism. Another dear friend, Lori Macek, began the cover design work as well as the interior artwork.

The rest of the tribe consists of: Amy M., Amy O., Kay, Kathy, Beth, Ruth Ann, Missy, Laura, Suzanne, Sally, Dawn, Rene, Gretchen, Mari Clare, Lyn, Traci, Chris, Julie, Kelly, Joelle, Susan, Jo, Kelly, Michelle, and Sue. I'm so blessed! Thank you for helping me with the decisions and the support along the way!

Introduction

Do you enjoy inspirational quotes? I remember having them plastered around my room in high school and college. It began when I came across a quote in a magazine that spoke to my soul, and I cut it out. I had a cork wall where I would pin these quotes. Many of them even traveled to college with me in a folder. The folder got larger over the years, and whenever I came across it, I would take some time to ponder and reflect upon these quotes. After I got married and had children, I just didn't have the time to look at them. Then, as a Licensed Clinical Professional Counselor, I found myself providing my clients with insights and phrases I thought would improve their quality of life. Over ten years ago, I decided to combine my folder of inspirations with my own "words of wisdom" and share them with friends in a weekly email with the hope of providing them ideas to contemplate and put into practice. What follows is a compilation of some of those inspirations, broken up into fifty-two weeks and including quotes by others as well as myself. I encourage you to reflect on each theme. These quotes and thoughts are meant to help you stay focused on the positive aspects of life. After each week, you are provided with a blank page to write yourself a message, draw a picture, glue down a photo, or include anything else to make that positive message personal for you.

I have created an Inspiration for you to reflect upon each week of the year. At the end of each section, you will also find a question or two, or a challenge.

Enjoy! May your year be filled with new thoughts and inspiration toward a more fulfilling life.

Week One | Today is a New Day

Life is not a bowl of cherries. Sometimes all we see are the pits. When life gives you lemons, make lemonade. The point is that we have situations presented to us each day, and we have the choice to either see the pits or turn them into something positive.

When we are confronted with a challenge, we can either let it overwhelm us and bring us to a discouraged frame of mind, or we can plow forward, even if it is a little step at a time. While we do not have control over people and circumstances, we can control how we react to them. (If you do struggle with controlling your response to a particular situation, I encourage you to reach out to a professional for help!)

With each new day, we have a new opportunity to set the course of our day and our future. Then the next day, we have the same opportunity.

Today is a new day, tomorrow is too!
—Geri A. Condon

As we wake up each new morning, we can reset ourselves. Recommit to your goals for that day. You don't have to look further. And then at the end of the day, let go of your struggles. Let them float away as you drift off to sleep.

As each day offers a fresh start, the next day offers the same! We can put our efforts into the present and leave tomorrow until tomorrow.

May you live each day to its fullest!

Focus

As you go through this week, I challenge you to start each day with a focus on JUST the day ahead of you. Journal, draw, or take a picture to remind yourself about being present in this day.

Journal or Draw!

Week Two | *Renewed Friendships*

Now is a great time to reflect on what is working in our lives and what is not. The older I get, the more I can appreciate what I have, decipher what I am willing to tolerate, and decide what I am willing to do and accept. From several diverse groups of friends, I hear the same thing. We have "put in our time," and now it's time for us to focus on ourselves and what makes us happy. While this may sound selfish at first, on reflection, it is taking ownership of the direction in which we want our lives to go.

For me, I find that what really makes me happy is spending time with my friends. For many years, happiness was about raising my kids. Now I am spending time with my friends, and these women rejuvenate me. Time with them makes me what and who I want to be.

If I could sit across the porch from God, I'd thank Him for lending you to me.
—Flavia

Take time to let your friends know how much you value their presence in your life. They are a gift.

May you know the worth of friendship!

Focus

This week's focus is on friendship. Reach out to one or more friends you haven't spoken to for a while. Using the space on the next page, list the friends you want to reach out to, add pictures of you and them, or write down the qualities you admire in their friendship.

Friend Appreciation Week!

-
-
-
-
-
-

Week Three | *Being Gracious*

I once went to a high school event on diversity. Of the five speakers, two were students who had seen others judge their friends and family and understood how cruel and devastating that can be. There was also a musician who had been partially blind from a young age yet excelled in so many areas, and a woman who received a death threat because she wanted to move for a job but was not accepted because of the color of her skin. Finally, there was a coach who was hired in a predominantly white community and faced racial slurs. But he loved the kids so much. His team was looking at a 42-0 shutout season. But during one game, the opposing team had a person with a cognitive disability who had never been on the field. This coach encouraged his players to make way for this player to score a touchdown. These five people are examples for us all. Sometimes it is easy to do the right thing, and other times it is not. Doing the right thing is always the best course of action. Even if you are angry or frustrated, you will feel better if you do the right thing.

Be pretty if you can, be witty if you must, but be gracious if it kills you.
—Elsie de Wolfe

The word *gracious* is defined by dictionary.com as "pleasantly kind, benevolent, and courteous." It is not always easy to be gracious, but it is a wonderful "look" on all of us. If you are gracious, you are pretty!

May your path be filled with gracious moments and gracious faces!

Focus

On the next page, consider ways you can be gracious. How does it make you feel when you choose to be gracious to others?

Journal Time!

Week Four | Internal Strength

We have all had struggles, with addictions, finances, parenting, illness, grief, relationships, and the list goes on. Even if you need to see a physician or therapist, there are two things that seem to help through these challenging times: faith in God and a reliance on friends. To function in the midst of adversity also requires us to look within and rely upon ourselves to choose to survive through the struggle.

Strength does not come from physical capacity. It comes from an indomitable will.
—Mahatma Gandhi

When I set my mind on something, I move forward and carry on. Of course, I often hit roadblocks, but when I do, I alter the path a little. For example, my intention to write this book has been many years in the making. While the concepts were clear to me, the outline was not. Once it was written, I needed to consider publishing options and hit roadblock after roadblock. I could have given up the dream, but after years of writing, months of searching for a publisher, and a disappointment in the timeline I had set for myself, this book is finally in your hands. The lesson is to just keep moving. Do not settle, and do not stagnate. Remember that mind over matter does make a difference. Moving forward may mean full force, or it may mean just a tiny budge. Do not wait for life to happen. Instead, be part of the movement of your life.

May you find strength of will along your path so that you can move pebbles and even mountains!

Focus

Is there something that you feel challenged with, whether it's physically, emotionally, professionally, or something else? Consider the challenge, and on the next page, write down ways you can take steps (not leaps, just little, individual steps) toward making a difference. Maybe you just need to say to yourself, "I can do this!" Now write that down!

I can do this!

Week Five | Be Elegant

Joy and beauty are all around us (the chirping of robins, the flowers poking through the earth, the smiles of children, the cuddling of dogs), but there is also so much suffering. It would be easy to ask "Why?" Does the why really matter, though? Shouldn't the question be "What are we going to do about the situation?" Whether we are dealing with parenting, financial difficulties, loss of loved ones, illness, etc., we need to choose how we respond. Do you want to give up or give in, or do you choose to steadfastly move forward? You may not have had any choice in what you have been dealt in life, but you can choose how you respond to these situations.

Surviving is important. Thriving is elegant.
—Maya Angelou

While surviving is important, **how** we survive is also important. So many horrible situations across the world arise because people have chosen to retaliate against their fellow mankind. I recently heard of a mother who had one son die of an overdose and another by gang fire. She now goes around speaking against these terrible killers. While she could have stayed in her misery, she chose to use her agony to help others. She **is** thriving elegantly! Sometimes just putting a smile on your face can be thriving elegantly. Don't we all feel better when we see a smile? It gives hope to the future.

May your path be filled with surviving, thriving, and smiling!

Focus

Use the next page to explore how you can survive a challenge you are facing while proceeding with elegance rather than anger, frustration, or whatever other negative emotion is brewing. Or paste down a picture of someone you admire who reminds you of how they have survived with elegance.

Explore & Reflect

Week Six | *Friendship*

I have been very blessed with many friendships over the years. Some have come and gone, while others have stayed constant throughout my life, even when we do not see each other regularly or talk often. There are numerous studies and statistics about how important friendship is to your mental health, but the real proof is in how it makes you feel. The words and actions of a true friend will lift you up. This does not mean a friendship does not need effort and commitment. Anything worthwhile requires these!

"Friendship," said Christopher Robin, "is a very comforting thing to have."—A. A. Milne

I have always loved Winnie the Pooh, and Christopher Robin is just charming. They always see the good in each other and are always there to help each other through a crisis. True friendship is being sensitive to each other's needs, even when you need to hear something hard. Friends soften the challenging times and offer their love and compassion.

We all have rough, tough, challenging times in our lives. What helps us through may be different for each person, but friends help along the way. After having gone through some heart-wrenching weeks, a childhood friend, a college roommate, and a friend from post-college all unexpectedly called me. I thought it divine providence that these three dear friends reached out to me when I needed them. They did not know that I needed them, and really, even I did not know that I needed them. But there they were to remind me of better times and encourage me for better future times. Their mere voices gave me strength.

Sprinkle your life with friendships and gather them when needed!
—Geri A. Condon

As humans go, we are all so much more alike than different. And although our circumstances may be different, we often have similar life experiences. In both the good and the bad, we need to draw strength and comfort from each other. Sometimes it is just the mere voice of a friend that sprinkles your life with love, comfort, and hope. I have been blessed by my friends, and I wish the same for you.

May you be accompanied by comforting friends along your life's journey!

Focus

On the next few pages, write down the name of a friend who you instantly turn to when you need a hug (even if it is virtual), sound advice, or just an ear to listen to you vent. Have you ever shared with her/him how important they are to you? Write about how important they are to you, then send them a note letting them know.

Hey, Friend

Week Seven | *Cleaning House*

One of the responsibilities of being a grown-up includes keeping your house clean. When you look around your home and see cobwebs, you need to get to work.

You also need to keep your HOUSE clean. By HOUSE, I mean within yourself! You need to shake up the mental cobwebs. Whether you do some spring cleaning or fall cleaning, it is a positive exercise to look around you, your home, your responsibilities, and your health to see if you need to make some adjustments and freshen things up! This exercise will help you determine where you focus your energy so that your HOUSE stays clean!

1. What activities am I committed to?
2. Which of these activities do I enjoy?
3. Which of these activities would I be willing to let go?
4. Are there new activities I would like to explore?
5. Is the space in which I surround myself cluttered or clear?
6. Do I need to implement/assess my exercise routines?
7. When am I most productive?
8. Am I getting the nutrients/vitamins I need?

You may have additional questions—write them down. Do an inventory of yourself and your surroundings at least once a year, but twice is better! It helps you stay fresh and clean. Use the next page (you might need additional paper!) to record your answers. Then reflect on whether you were surprised by any of your answers. Make a priority list of what changes you would like to implement to get your HOUSE cleaned!

Priority List

-
-
-
-
-
-
-
-
-
-
-

Time to Clean House!

Week Eight | *Silence is Golden*

Bigger, faster, bolder. We are in an age of speed and accessibility. Adults juggle home, work, and play; kids juggle school, home, sports, and other activities. Rarely do we stop to smell the flowers, or even take note that there are flowers. We rush from one activity to the next. And silence—is there such a thing? Noise is all around us.

Find serenity in silence.
—Geri A. Condon

There is a lot to be gained from a little silence—a clearing of the mind! It is more common to be overwhelmed and racing than it is to be silent. Giving yourself the gift of silence, even if it is only for five minutes each day, can be cleansing. We cleanse our physical bodies almost every day, but rarely do we consider the need to cleanse our minds. By seeking a little silence, you will be more clearheaded and fresh of mind, and maybe you even will see and smell those flowers!

May you find a little silence along your path this week!

Focus

Use the next page to draw or adhere a peaceful, serene location. Imagine yourself there with no cell phone or other distractions. How do you feel? What are you thinking about? Journal a little about this silent time!

My Peaceful Place

Week Nine

Do Not Give Your Consent

So often we look for other people's reactions to what we say, wear, or do. We all want to be validated, but sometimes we give so much credibility to others that we do ourselves a disservice.

No one can make you feel inferior without your consent.
—Eleanor Roosevelt

That saying has gotten me through insecure moments in college, business, and interactions with friends and is a guiding mantra for me. I am not willing to give my consent to others over what I know is best for me.

A client of mine saw the above quote in my office. She stated, "That is very hard to do." I thought about that for a while and came to this conclusion: It is hard to not seek and desire approval from others. We all innately want to be accepted. But often the cost is too great. If all you want is to fit in, are you being true to yourself? Maybe, but often not. If I stand up for myself and feel good about my decisions, then the consent of others is worthless. Of course, the assumption here is that one has self-confidence in the first place.

I try to be self-confident. But either way, I know I do not want to give my consent, approval, or power to any other human being to determine my self-worth.

May you gather self-worth along your path!

Focus

Take some time and journal on the next few pages about your own self-confidence. Have you given consent to others about your self-worth? If so, how can you take it back? If you struggle with this, ask a close friend whom you trust to help you see yourself through her/his eyes.

I am enough.

Week Ten

What an Opportunity!

We all face challenges, disappointments, losses, and struggles. They often occur not of our own doing, and we have no choice in their origin. We do, however, have a choice on how we address these challenges.

All your problems, discouragements, and heartaches
are in truth great opportunities in disguise.
—Og Mandino

While you may wish you did not get into a car accident, you might be excited about getting a new car. While you may not like the doctor telling you to lose weight, you might like not taking blood pressure medication anymore. While you may be discouraged about not getting the job you wanted, you might appreciate a more productive path that's just around the corner.

The key to benefitting from available opportunities is to SEE them and not have your vision clouded by these challenges, disappointments, losses, and struggles! Of course, this is easier said than done when you are in the midst of pain, loss, or other struggle. After some time has passed, though, you may be able to look at the situation and see something you can take away as a positive.

May your path provide opportunities after a challenge,
and may you have the vision to see them!

Focus

On the next page, journal about whether you primarily focus, and often become stuck, on the negative circumstances of your life or if you try to see the silver lining. Imagine what it would look like to "see" the opportunity, even in challenging circumstances. How would that make you feel? How would it motivate you to move forward?

Reflect & Move Forward

Week Eleven

Broken, but Not Out

So many times, awful things happen in our lives, and we just want to know why. Why me? Why this? Why now? Even if we had the answers, though, it would not change what we are facing. How the story continues is up to you. You can let the situation break you, or you can find the inner strength to learn and thrive.

Things don't go wrong and break your heart so you can become bitter and give up.
They happen to break you down and build you up so you
can be all that you were intended to be.
—Charlie Jones

Stand up, brush off the past, learn a lesson, and move forward! Your story and situation are in your hands. You can stay down and be broken, or you can stand up and rebuild!

May your path find you refining and rebuilding all that has been broken!

Focus

On the next page, draw something that is broken, even as simple as a circle where the ends do not meet. Then draw something that is complete, like a closed circle. Which one holds more strength? Now go to the first item and complete it. Let that visual remind you that you have the power to rebuild and repair what feels broken!

Time to Draw!

Week Twelve

The Challenge of Change

Most people do not like change. It can be stressful and burdensome. Like it or not, we are faced with changes every day. Seasons come and go, we grow older, we are exposed to new ideas, new technology, and so on. We can be open and adapt, or we can fight our way through like a two-year-old having a tantrum. Battling the change before you only makes it harder, both mentally and physically. Being open to new possibilities and opportunities, though, can broaden and enrich our lives.

Change is never painful. Only resistance to change is painful.
—Buddha

The more we resist, the more challenging it becomes. While change may not be easy, it does not have to be difficult either. As humans, we can adapt. Do not waste your time and energy on fighting inevitable changes, but rather embrace the journey. Seek the positive and move forward.

May your path find you embracing change and seeing where the new path takes you!

Focus

On the next page, journal about a time when you had to make a change in your life (moving out of your parents' home, starting a new job, dealing with a health situation, etc.). Then decide if you embraced the change or if you were resistant. If you were resistant, how might it have been different if you had a mindset of acceptance?

Embrace Change

Week Thirteen

The Mark of Your Journey

Each of us walks a different journey. Our childhood neighborhood, our first place of employment, the first place we called our own, vacation spots, and everywhere else we have traveled are locations unique to us alone. These places play a part in our development and who we ultimately become.

Each part of the world has a unique character, and these characteristics impact who we become: our values, assumptions, and philosophies. The family dynamics of our home do the same thing. Do you live with two parents? Are you an only child? Our physical landscape, such as a big city, an open countryside, or a body of water, all leave their mark upon us and shape who we become.

Wherever you go becomes a part of you somehow.
—Anita Desai

The more we resist, the more challenging it becomes. While change may not be easy, it does not have to be difficult either. As humans, we can adapt. Do not waste your time and energy on fighting inevitable changes, but rather embrace the journey. Seek the positive and move forward.

May your path take you to places you can treasure and from which you can learn!

Focus

On the next few pages, write down all the places where you have lived, worked, and traveled to, as well as the cultures you have encountered. Which did you like best? Which did you like least?

Oh, the Places You've Gone

Week Fourteen
The Power of the Mind

What messages do you hear in your mind? Our thoughts tend to validate us, both the positive and the negative. If the same message is being replayed in our mind, we tend to believe it as truth, which then dictates our words and actions.

The mind is everything. What you think you become.
—Buddha

What consumes your mind, controls your life.
—Unknown

Consider if you were told that you were worthless and would not find success or happiness. If the message was repeated, your mind might take it as truth, and you might give up trying to do any better. What if you were told repeatedly that you were bright and loveable and successful? Would that not motivate you to continue that path?

You have the option of removing yourself from negative messages and thoughts. And you can purposefully fill your mind with positive messages. For example, start your day with a positive affirmation, quote, or even perspective for the day. Your mind will then be drawn toward seeking that positive message throughout the day. Maybe you have not found your success yet, but if you focus your mind on moving forward, your actions will follow.

Let your mind lead you in the direction you want to pursue!

Focus

On the next page, write down the message you want to hear in your mind. Then repeat that message to yourself each day. You will be changing your mindset!

A Message to Self

Week Fifteen | *Hope*

When things look sad, bad, or scary in our lives, we need to believe that things can and do change. That is called HOPE.

Where flowers bloom, so does HOPE.
—Lady Bird Johnson

What a wonderful vision! Flowers grow from little seeds that look rather dull and worthless. But as they grow into beautiful flowers, you see the change as something valuable. The change from seed to flower can be a sign for us. Out of something that must be buried can rise something extraordinary. We need to all have hope for a better tomorrow!

You too, with hope for transformation, can grow and learn and become something beyond your pain and suffering. Encountering life's challenges is inevitable. It is the gift of hope that can motivate you to move past them and not get stuck in their muck. So, bloom away!

May your path be filled with blooms and hope!

Focus

On the next page, either paste down a picture of a beautiful flower or draw your own flower. Let it remind you that a seed buried will blossom over time. Write about how you might need to "bury" a part of yourself (let go of a past hurt) so you can transform into something more beautiful (a life more hopeful)!

Time to Draw!

Week Sixteen | *Canvas of Life*

There is so much beauty in our world. Of course, the ugly often stands out, but if you really look around, you can see the beauty. A bird's nest is made of twigs, grass, and other discarded material, but within it we can find the miracle of a newborn robin. The canvas of the Grand Canyon may not be in your backyard, but most likely you can find awe-inspiring wonder if you look! And what about you? You can also be a canvas of creativity and beauty!

Life is a great big canvas. Throw all the paint you can at it.
—Danny Kaye

Live outside the lines and bring beauty and creativity into your life. If you pass by these opportunities, you are not tapping into the opportunities life offers.

May your path be one giant canvas that you fill with wonder and love!

Focus

On the next page, find pictures of things you find beautiful and paste them down. Then remember to look for them all around you!

Collage

Week Seventeen

When you feel STUCK in any or all aspects of your life, it is likely you feel alone, lost, and in the dark. It may feel like a long, dark tunnel with no light ahead, so you bump around trying to move but do not make any progress.

The first step to lighting the way is to recognize that you are stuck in the dark. The second is to get the resources you need to make progress. What you have been doing is not working. If you want things to be better or different, you need to do something different. You need to change.

It is better to light a candle than curse the darkness.
—William Watkinson

Time to buy some candles! Maybe you need to see a doctor, therapist, or other professional. Sometimes we just do not have the skills within us and need those who are experts to come in and light the way.

May you find ways to brighten your path!

Focus

On the next few pages, write down areas in your life where you may be "in the dark" or stuck. Then next to them, jot down resources that may help light your way.

Week Eighteen | *Being Bold*

As a woman, I believed I needed to be a little bold to get my point of view recognized in my initial career of government service, which was a male-dominated arena. That inner gut instinct to stand tall (and for someone who is only 5'1", that is a feat in itself!), exude confidence (even when you do not feel it), and move forward is sometimes the correct and even only way to be acknowledged. But it is not always the most appropriate way!

Be bold in a healthy way.
—Amy Layton

Sometimes you can be bold with a gentle, quiet voice of reason. Sometimes your silence is "speaking" boldly. The bottom line is that we need to know when it is appropriate to be loud and when to be quiet. Being bold comes from within. It is our desire to be passionately heard, even if there is an element of personal risk. You may need to get the attention of others, so a loud voice and message is required. Other times, your point can be made by speaking slowly and quietly. Knowing your audience is important.

May your path be filled with your boldness in loud and quiet ways!

Focus

On the next few pages, journal about your own personal journey and whether you are typically bold in loud or quiet ways. Then reflect on whether you are more comfortable in the loud or quiet ways. Are they effective? Do you need to increase your confidence in being bold?

Reflect

Week Nineteen

Changing Decorations Both Inside and Out

With each season comes new changes. In spring, the bright colors of flowers pop; in summer, we feel the warmth; in fall, we see the leaves on the trees change color; and winter brings along snowy white backdrops and cold. As the "decorations" in our backyard change, we too need to change our decorations from time to time, both inside and out.

Know, first, who you are, and then adorn yourself accordingly.
—Epictetus

This surely means putting on a smile, but I also think it can mean changing our wardrobes. Find your style and immerse yourself in it. It can also mean a reflection on what you value. What brings you joy? What is weighing down your heart, and what is lifting you up? Truly get to know who you are, what you want, and where you are going, and then surround yourself with those things and go in those directions.

May your adornments begin with your smile and radiate outward!

Focus

On the next page, take some time to consider your style and write it down, or find some pictures of the styles you are trying to create in your life and paste them in.

What's My Style?

Week Twenty
Who Completes You?

In the movie *Jerry Maguire*, Jerry, played by Tom Cruise, says to Renée Zellweger's character, "You complete me." It was the pinnacle of the movie, and yes, it made me cry!

Although it was a great sentiment in the movie, I hope you can say that you complete yourself. Sure, my family is part of what completes me, as are my work, my friends, and so on. Ultimately, though, it is up to me to complete myself. To take it one step further, I think we are all *works in progress* and are never complete. As life changes, you need to adapt and, therefore, are always evolving.

I'm a work in progress.
—Geri A. Condon

There are people, situations, and events that move us in the direction of progress throughout life. Those are the things in life with which we want to surround ourselves. You cannot rely on any one person or thing to make you complete, but you can fill your life with those that make you better, happier. And it is up to you to direct that course!

May you complete your life along with a few trusted cheerleaders!

Focus

On the next few pages, jot down the ways you have changed over the years. Do you like the ways in which you have changed? Who are the people who support you? Do you need to include more supporters?

How have I changed?

Week Twenty-one

Smile

Some days it is easier to smile than others. Sometimes we need to fake the smile when inside we feel like screaming. And some days we see people smile, and before we know it, we are smiling too!

We shall never know all the good that a simple smile can do.
—Mother Teresa

That quote from Mother Teresa was on a calendar with pictures of children with special needs. Alongside the quote from Mother Teresa was a quote from one of the children:

…my grandma says my smile is contagious and it can change someone's day!—Heather

How wise is Heather?! Not only do we feel better when we smile, we can start a chain reaction of smiles. Have you ever noticed that when you smile at someone, they often smile back? You have touched that person. I suspect you changed their day as much as the smile changed you. A smile is a gift we can freely give and give and give!

Our smile to others is certainly a gift to them, but it can be a gift to ourselves as well. I have had great joy and great sorrow in my life. Who hasn't? The great thing about our existence is that at the end of each day, we close our eyes to what we have just completed. Later, we awake to a fresh start and a new beginning. Although our trials and tribulations may not have gone away overnight, we do have a new opportunity to face them, well rested and with new vigor. There are so many quotes about the end of a day, such as "Don't go to bed mad at each other" or "Kiss each other good night." I like this:

Close the door on this day…

We cannot redo a day, nor can we change what has already passed. So, try not to dwell on what has already happened. That does not mean your worries and problems go away, but there is no use in fretting over what cannot be relived. The quote above continues:

...open tomorrow with a smile.—Geri A. Condon

No matter what lies ahead of you with each new day, it can only be enhanced with a smile, both for yourself and for others. Any struggles you may encounter may seem a little less of a burden, and the joys may be more enhanced. Yes, it is subtle, but it can start your day off in a way that may unfold into a brighter outcome.

May you smile each day!

Focus

Upon waking each day, remember to smile. It can change your mindset for the day. Then on the next two pages, journal about how your life has been touched by a smile from someone.

May your path be filled with smiles given and received!

Touched by a Smile

Week Twenty-two
Letting Go and Holding On

Change is hard, and we are creatures of habit. Life gives us the opportunity to hold on to the lessons we have learned from the past as we move forward. It also allows us to let go of the past so we can grow and become who we are meant or want to be. The challenge is in knowing what to let go of and what to hold on to.

All the art of living lies in a fine mingling of letting go and holding on.
—Havelock Ellis

Often our head understands this, but our heart struggles. The key is to find balance between lessons learned from the past and letting go of what's holding us from making progress. When I hear that someone has gone through a particularly challenging life event, I ask them what they learned from the experience. Usually that catches them off guard, as they are merely trying to get through the situation. If you can find something positive about the experience, as challenging or as painful as it is, then your focus changes. You can let go of the pain but hold on to the lesson learned.

I saved much of my children's school artwork, papers, report cards, and awards. In my mind, I was saving it for them. But as adults, they do not want it. While I want them to want it, I realize they do not have the sentimental attachment to it that I do. So, I will keep a few (and I really mean a few) items for me and let go of the rest. You too can find the balance between what holds meaning and what should be let go.

May your path include a balance between holding on and letting go!

Focus

On the next few pages, write about what you might be holding on to that no longer serves a purpose. You might want to consider why you are holding on so tight. Then make a plan to let go of what no longer serves you!

Week Twenty-three

More Change

If you don't like how things are, change it! You're not a tree.
—Jim Rohn

When I first came upon this quote, I laughed out loud. Of course, change is easier said than done, but the point is that we are capable of change. While a tree may change by the season, it cannot change its location. We can! We just need to take a step and go out on that limb.

I do not want to think that any of us are wasting our time stuck in an uncomfortable place, relationship, job, or career. Take some time to reflect on all aspects of your life and determine whether you need a change. I am not suggesting any rash decisions, but rather a lingering reflection on where you are right now. If you are happy and content, great! If not, start considering possibilities. That is the first step. Then take whatever steps necessary to get to where you want to go.

May you realize your path has no end,
and you can switch directions whenever you want!

Focus

On the next page, draw or adhere a picture of a tree. Imagine yourself standing next to this tree, then take a step away from it. List the "steps" you need to take to move forward!

My tree...

Next steps...

-
-
-
-
-
-

Week Twenty-four | *Remember*

The phrase "9/11" brings many in our country right back to the moment when time seemed to stand still. Most people have a story to tell about what they were doing early on that day in 2001. I was getting my children ready for school and had the television on, listening but not really watching. But something caught my attention…a plane, a building, and fire. I sat down mesmerized by the newscasters discussing the plane that flew into one of the Twin Towers. As I was watching, I called a friend to talk about it. We watched in shock and horror as the next tower was attacked. After speaking to my kids about this tragedy, I took them to school. I stood in line with them while waiting to go into the school on that warm, sunny day and watched as a couple of planes flew overhead. Little did I know that we would not see a plane flying again for days.

We have always been a proud country, yet also have sought a peaceful existence both here and abroad. But on that day, those who tried to break our peaceful existence saw that we did not break as our resolve stood strong and we united. They woke us from an easygoing existence, yes, but also woke the proud, protective side of our country that will not tolerate fanaticism. Many died because of the cowardly acts of fanatics. Many more have died in the years since then trying to protect our freedom and develop freedom abroad. Politics and opinions aside, we need to reflect and honor those who have been wounded and killed because of this tragedy.

Reflect, pray, and carry on. Individually and collectively, we take note of this day. We nod our heads to the police officer who drives by. We hug our children a little tighter. We say the Pledge of Allegiance with a little more pride and enthusiasm.

Remember!

No famous author here, just my wish and hope of inspiring you to never forget.

May you remember as you move down your path!

Focus

On the next page, list the important events in your life, the ones that have helped define who you are. Do you hold these moments in your mind and heart? Remember that these events are a part of you!

Life-Defining Moments

-
-
-
-
-
-
-
-
-
-
-

Week Twenty-five | *Reaction*

Living in Illinois, you experience all four seasons. You can even experience the temperatures of two seasons in one day! You always need to be prepared. Day by day, day to day, things change. While change is inevitable, it is how we react that can determine how we weather the change.

Life is 10% what happens to you and 90% how you react to it.
—Charles Swindoll

I have both embraced what life has presented and fought the fight. Haven't we all? But life has taught me that it is easier and—in the long run, scary or not—more pleasant to embrace it and move forward than to ignore what we will have to face one day or another anyway. For example, when my husband's business was hit hard by an economic downfall, I had no choice but to downscale our expenses. I could be upset and feel cheated by my circumstances, or I could recognize that this was what I was amid and adapt. I do not want to waste one day of my life feeling helpless, miserable, or powerless. I CHOOSE to react to what happens to me. It really is a choice. I hope you choose to embrace life, good and bad, move forward, and handle all that life presents.

**May you choose to move forward along your path,
embracing all that comes your way!**

Focus

Take some time to reflect on how you typically react to change. On the next page, journal about those reactions. Do you fight change or embrace it, or both? Write down a time you fought change and how it would have been different if you had embraced the change.

My Thoughts on Change

Week Twenty-six | *Choose Good*

Have you ever been in a situation where most people involved were heading down a destructive path? You knew better, but that mob mentality was pulling you along…

When things go bad, don't go with them.
—Elvis Presley

You have a choice. Choosing the right thing is often hard when others are taking the easy way out. Know yourself, honor your values, be convicted, and stand strong. Then you will find it easy to go forward on the path to goodness no matter what others choose to do. It is a choice. Choose wisely!

May you choose the path toward goodness!

Focus

On the next few pages, jot down your top ten values. Then spend some time reflecting on how you live them out in your life. The stronger you are in your convictions, the easier it is to stay true to what you believe.

The Important Things

Week Twenty-seven | *Believe*

My dad taught me to believe in myself, and if I did that, I could achieve success. I have a tattoo on my left wrist to remind myself to Believe. Personally, I believe in myself and that God has a purpose for me. That said, I am a continual work in progress, and my purpose has changed throughout the years. I am a wife, mother, daughter, friend, counselor, etc. Whatever my pursuit, I believe I will achieve, or at the very least make a difference.

Believe like there's endless possibilities.
—Unknown

I do believe we all have endless possibilities. Of course, we may stumble and fall, but we can get back up and learn a lesson. We just need to believe in ourselves to achieve, overcome, persevere, and do it all with confidence.

So many take a weak approach when they start something new, and their actions are covered in doubt. I challenge you to see, believe in, and focus on the possibilities. When you set your mind on the positive, you are more driven and likely to see them!

May you see the possibilities along your path!

Focus

On the next few pages, journal about your possibilities. As you write, envision your successes! You will be one step closer to achieving your dreams.

The possibilities are endless!

Week Twenty-eight
Create Your Life

I have had many different jobs throughout my life: bank employee, state capitol staffer, licensed counselor. Even as I get older, though, I continue to think (and say), "I don't know what I want to be when I grow up."

Then again, I refuse to grow up. Yes, my body is growing older every day, but mentally, I hope to always see things through the eyes of a child. They always see the wonder of possibility!

Life isn't about finding yourself. Life is about creating yourself.
—George Bernard Shaw

Within us are our individual goals, insights, and dreams. We can hope they come our way, or we can seek them. Actively moving ourselves toward what we want allows us the means to create our reality. We have the luxury of being the director of our destiny. We get to CREATE who we are both internally and externally. So, go get creative!

May you create your path of life as you choose to live it!

Focus

On the next few pages, make a list of all the things you would like to accomplish, places you'd like to visit, and anything else you are looking forward to in your lifetime.

Bucket List Time

-
-
-
-
-
-
-
-
-
-
-

Week Twenty-nine | *Choose to Rise*

Life is sometimes funny. One day, you are sailing through it, doing okay, and then wham!—all chaos breaks out. Or you are in a miserable situation and a rainbow suddenly shows you a new direction. We never really know what is before us. We plan and prepare, but there is no guarantee that things will work out in the way we plan. That does not mean we should not plan and prepare, but we should always be ready for the unexpected and embrace limitless opportunities too!

We will all be "tested" in life. We will be challenged to our very core. It is how we face or hide from these challenges that will determine whether we adapt and grow or hide and wither.

I grew up in a small community where everyone knew each other and knew each other's business. My senior year in college, I had gotten a call from a hometown friend who told me my father was leaving my mom. True enough, my parents divorced, and my father married the woman he had been seeing. My dad was my idol, and his infidelity opened my eyes to the reality that he was a mere mortal. I felt all eyes upon myself and my family. I cried, I raged, I rose my head up and carried on. After many years, I can say that my dad, his wife, and I now have an amazing relationship, and I feel blessed to have my stepmom in my life!

Life will present us with situations where
we will stumble and fall: Choose to rise and carry on.
—Geri A. Condon

It is inevitable that you will be challenged along the path of life. Some will let the chaos and frustrations overcome them. They will all sink down at times. But know that you do have a choice. And I hope you choose to rise, dust off the dirt, and keep going. Find the strength from within and rise a little taller than before, a little stronger than before, and smile!

May you always choose to rise
and persevere as you journey along your path!

Focus

Reflect upon your past and recall the times that you were challenged, yet you persevered. Write those down. Also note how you felt about overcoming and moving forward. When challenging times come your way again, remember that you have been able to pull through before and rely upon your strength!

I am an overcomer.

Week Thirty

The Gift of an Hour

What have you done for yourself today? Or rather, I should ask, when was the last time you did something for yourself?

This is an important question. If you are not taking care of yourself, you will not have it in you to help others! Remember the script from the flight attendant on the airplane about putting the oxygen mask on yourself before you put it on anyone else?

Years ago, a dear friend of mine gave me an hourglass. At first, I thought it was an odd gift, especially from someone who knows me well and seems to always give me a perfect gift. After I thanked her for the gift, she asked if I knew the significance. I honestly said I had no idea. She explained that she was giving me the gift of an hour, knowing that I am busy and often focused on others instead of myself. She suggested I use this timer for an hour to enjoy myself, do something creative, read a book, or whatever I might need to replenish myself.

What a remarkable gift! I just needed to put it into practice. I now keep the hourglass close at hand, and while I do not use it every day, I do treat myself on occasion!

I wish you an hour of sand!
—Geri A. Condon

While you may not have an hourglass (though I encourage you to get one!), you can take an hour to replenish, rejuvenate, rest, or whatever else you might need to engage the best version of yourself. Get yourself an hourglass. Give yourself an hour. See how good you feel.

May your path be filled with hours of time spent on yourself!

Focus

On the next page, make a list of things you would do with a "free" hour to enjoy. Now, go do one!

What to do?

-
-
-
-
-
-
-
-
-
-
-

Week Thirty-one

Go About Your Business – Follow Your Dreams

Do you have a passion? Is it a hobby, or your job, or a calling? My own passion has changed over the years, along with two distinct career directions. I believe that we all have something that draws our attention and nudges us along. And often that "passion" changes. The important thing is to pay attention. What is drawing your attention? Are you following it? Seeking it? Practicing it?

Oprah had a passion with her television show, but after twenty-five years, she was nudged in a new direction. On her last show, she asked and answered the following:

What are you called to do? Get about the business of doing it.—Oprah Winfrey

I have reframed her words to:

What is your business? Are you going about it?
—Geri A. Condon

Look at what draws your attention. Are you spending time there, or are you stuck elsewhere? Do you have a "nudging" feeling? It is scary to consider leaving what we know to follow our dreams and passions. It requires us to go outside of our comfort zone.

We can waste a lot of time and energy on just getting through life, or we can follow our dreams and passions. I encourage you to go forth and do your business. And enjoy!

May your path lead you in the direction of your passion!

Focus

On the next few pages, journal about your passions. Ask yourself if you are being led to do something different. Then journal about how your life would be different if you were to pursue your passion.

What is my passion?

Week Thirty-two | *Be Flexible*

Life often throws us curveballs, and we are faced with challenges we did not anticipate.

Women are angels, and when someone breaks our wings, we simply continue to fly on a broomstick—We are flexible that way!
—Unknown

I laughed so hard when I first read this quote. But there is some truth in it! I tend to merrily go along, but when someone ruffles my feathers (or wings!), I will defend myself, my family, my community, and so on.

But the real lesson from this quote is that we should be flexible. Like it or not, we will enjoy life a lot more if we can gracefully transition ourselves when faced with adversity. In the quote above, the words "simply continue" are significant. When we are faced with a challenge, we should adapt and continue along. I wish I could say I do that easily, but often I do not. I would like to, though!

I encourage you to embrace whatever emotion you are facing. Keep moving, knowing flexibility is what will allow you to do that. Whether we're using wings or a broomstick, we need to continue to fly!

May you find your path even as you are flying above!

Focus

On the next page, journal about times in your life when you were flexible. Also recall times when you were not. What was different in both cases?

Flexibility

Week Thirty-three | *Opportunity*

Have you ever noticed how quickly things can turn around? One day it is sunny, the next it is raining. One day your child is home, the next they leave for college. One day you are in pain, the next you are healed. Of course, some changes occur more quickly than in a day, and some take much, much longer.

What a difference a day makes.
—Unknown

The best difference in each and every day is OPPORTUNITY! Each day offers us opportunity—opportunity to change! We should set our minds on the reality that when we open our eyes each morning, we are full of possibilities! That does not mean we can or should erase whatever sad or depressing thing that may have happened the day before, but we have a NEW opportunity to address it with a bright, hopeful, and positive mindset. It doesn't matter what we didn't get accomplished the day before because it is now behind us. Today, we can set things in motion. Each new day offers the potential of being different from the day before, but we must engage it and take the opportunities that it offers.

May you take time to see the opportunity that each new day allows!

Focus

On the next page, write down a message or a quote that you can use to remind yourself that each day offers a fresh start.

Message of the Day

Week Thirty-four | *Clean Mind*

Sometimes we are our own worst enemy. We get to doubting ourselves or questioning our choices. At other times, we allow others to infiltrate our mind and mess up the positive worth we have created within. We need to have good boundaries and a clear vision and direction of our thoughts and corresponding actions.

I will not let anyone walk through my mind with their dirty feet.
— Mahatma Gandhi

I do not like to get dirty. I avoid puddles so the water and mud do not dirty my legs. While I have been protective of not getting dirty physically, I never applied that concept to my mind.

Some people who are hurting spit out negatives toward others to make themselves feel better and not alone in their struggles. Some do not realize how their negativity impacts the people around them. These are just a couple of ways other people can "dirty" our mind. I am not talking about constructive criticism, which can be very helpful, but rather people who just muddy up our beliefs, thoughts, and perceptions.

When we are feeling positive and mentally healthy, we need to protect that mindset and keep it clean and clear. We can do that by surrounding ourselves with positive inspirations and positive people.

May your mind not be muddied up by others!

Focus

On the next page, draw a picture of dirty feet, or find an image of dirty feet and adhere it. Then draw or find an image of clean feet. Use it as a reminder to let go of the "dirty people" who you come across and stay focused on the positive people who can lift you out of your mindset!

Time to draw!

Week Thirty-five | *Age*

When I was a teenager, my aunt turned thirty. The adults all said she was depressed because of the number of her age. At the time, I could understand being upset that she was turning thirty. That seemed so old. Fast-forward, and the worst year of my life was when I was twenty-nine. I thought I had to have a lot of fun because when I turned thirty, my life would be over and all downhill. Well, I turned fifty a few years ago and am still going strong and having fun!

The number of our age does have an impact on us. When you turn sixteen, you can get a driver's license. When you turn twenty-one, you can legally drink alcohol. And when you turn fifty, you are eligible for the benefits of AARP.

Age is a number that has benefits for certain milestones, but it is just a number. It is how we live that really defines us! I have often said, "I refuse to grow up." I love glitter, giggle like a schoolgirl, and enjoy many of the same things I did when I was in my twenties. Yes, my body may have slowed me down, but I refuse to let any number rule my life.

Age is a number, not a definition.
— Geri A. Condon

Yes, life does seem to go by quicker as I get older. That just means I make time to see the good, smell the flowers, and not take my blessings for granted. Each day is a gift. Live your life to the fullest no matter your age, and do not let any number define who you are. Be you!

May your path keep you young at heart!

Focus

On the next page, list the birthdays that have been significant for you. Reflect and journal about any milestone birthdays that you are looking forward to or are apprehensive about. Write down your age now, the age you physically feel, the age you mentally feel, and the age you live out!

Age is just a number!

Week Thirty-six | *Take a Risk*

Although we sometimes need to be patient and wait, other times require us to act. If all we did was wait for life to get better, or a job to come along, or a friendship to develop, then we would probably wait forever. We must take action to make life's wishes become reality.

You've got to go out on a limb sometimes because that's where the fruit is.
— Will Rogers

The benefit of a life well lived is often worth going out on that limb! We need to stretch our imagination, our confidence, and our security. When we do so, we realize that there is more out there than we might have expected. While not all the "fruit" on the limb is savory, and we may have to go out on several risky limbs to gain the reward, it will be worth the stretch.

May you reach for the limbs with the best fruit as you travel your path!

Focus

On the next page, journal about yourself or someone you admire who took a risk and was rewarded. If you are writing about yourself, how did it feel? Are your dreams bigger than your fears? And if you are writing about someone you admire, how did the risk work out for them?

Risk & Reward

Week Thirty-seven | *Playtime*

Our world demands much from us. We have jobs, responsibilities, finances, and family that require our attention. But we also need playtime.

You can discover more about a person in an hour of play than in a year of conversation.
— Laura Moncur

You deserve playtime. And you will be better for it. Let go of those burdens and bask in your playtime. Recall the times in your childhood when you were carefree. It will bring you back to who you really are. What were your favorite activities when you were a child? What are they now? What does playtime mean to you?

Through being playful, you let others know the softer, carefree version of you. That may look different for different people, but you and others will know it by the smile on your face!

May your path find you playing as you go along your way!

Focus

On the next page, recall your childhood. List the activities you did during playtime, who you did them with, and how you felt. Do you recognize those feelings and emotions when "playing" now? Are there activities that you could engage in now that would remind you of childhood playtime?

Oh, to be a child again.

Week Thirty-eight
I've Got a Friend in Me

Some people have many friends in different aspects of their lives, while others have only a few close ones. The number of friends one has is not as important as the quality of them, but the most important friend each person should have is themselves!

Friendship with one's self is all important, because without it one cannot be friends with anyone else in the world.
— Eleanor Roosevelt

If we are not treating ourselves well, how can others expect us to treat them? By being loving, forgiving, generous, kind, and compassionate (the list can go on and on) to ourselves, we show others how we want to be treated and how they can expect to be treated by us.

I hope you take time each day to see what a valuable friend you have in yourself. I encourage you to also keep track of how well you treat yourself with the qualities you like to receive from and give to others.

May you find your path filled with friendships, starting with yourself!

Focus

On the next page, write down the characteristics you look for in a friend. Then list the characteristics that demonstrate how you show friendship. Finally, circle the ones that you show toward yourself. What is left on the lists? Do you need to be a better friend toward yourself?

Friendship. Oh, what a gift.

Week Thirty-nine
The Gift of a Giggle

Do you remember when you were little and would giggle? Not just laugh, but really giggle! Have you ever giggled so hard your stomach muscles hurt?

So often, as adults, we hold back our emotions and expressions. That comes from a lot of reasons, but mostly we do not want to draw attention to ourselves. But when we let our guard down and giggle away, it can feel so refreshing!

Life is often hard. Between the economy, relationships, disappointments, and challenges, it can be a struggle to find something to laugh about. But we need to laugh for our own well-being! We were created to know joy. So, seek the opportunities around you that bring you happiness and let out a little giggle. Then let it out a little more. Laugh so hard your stomach muscles start aching!

Giggle until you drop.
— Geri A. Condon

May your path be filled with giggles heard loud and far!

Focus

On the next page, write about a time when you had so much fun that you were laughing uncontrollably. Then adhere a picture of you smiling or laughing. When you are upset, remind yourself that you can giggle!

Week Forty
The Value of Time

When I was in third grade, my teacher said, "When you are young, time goes slowly, but the older you get, the faster time passes by." As any normal third-grader would do, I tucked that tidbit into the "she doesn't know what she's talking about" pile in my brain. Funny thing is that I remember very little about being in third grade except for that very wise statement!

Fast-forward four decades or so…I have relished the milestones of my three children's lives. The first day of school for each of them has always been etched a little deeper, and of course there are those photos to keep my memory intact! Although, in retrospect, each phase of schooling seemed to go by way too quickly; the high school years were especially a whirlwind. So many of my friends are now experiencing their "babies" getting married and having their own babies. Where have the years gone?

It feels like all I have done is blink and my children have graduated high school, college, and/or moved across the country to live on their own.

I blinked, and time passed by!
— Geri A. Condon

We all blink! That is why I want to remind you (and me!) that we need to cherish, really CHERISH, those little milestones along the journey of our lives. As hard, and at times extraordinary, as these experiences can be, they all drift away in a moment of time. Live in the moment and soak up the experience!

May you treasure every moment on your path before you blink!

Focus

On the following page, make a list of the most important times in your life. After you have completed the list, look at one, then blink, look at the next one, then blink, and do so for the entire list. That's how quickly these moments seem to go through your life. Now take a moment to reflect on how slowly you "blink" each day onward from today!

Blink!

•

•

•

•

•

•

•

•

•

•

•

Week Forty-one | *It's Raining*

I love the sight of children and adults happily prancing in the rain. I, however, always view rain as an inconvenience. I came across a quote, not once, but twice in one month. It weighed heavily on my mind after the first sighting, but after the second, I knew I needed to share…

Some people walk in the rain, others just get wet.
— Roger Miller

In the past, I would have instantly said that I get wet. But after experiencing some challenging years, I came to realize that I needed to seek the possibilities. So now, I prance. Well, in my mind I prance, but it is more like a lingering.

I am still getting wet, but I am appreciating the experience and (literally) soaking up the sensation. Rain is cleansing, refreshing, renewing. I need that. We all need that. I could either complain about the inconvenience or delight in the rain. I now choose to see the beauty of the rain, the gift from above, the change in the air. It's an opportunity to look at my surroundings a little differently and to become a little playful in the process. Don't we all need that? Rain can be the reminder to not take life so seriously and to embrace the present.

May you jump in the puddles along your path!

Focus

On the next page, either draw a picture of you walking, prancing, or enjoying some rain, or find a picture of yourself being playful, whimsical, or enjoying a funny moment and adhere it. Let this remind you to not take life too seriously!

Time to Draw!

Week Forty-two | *Keep Going...*

As a spiritual person, the saying that "God won't give you more than you can handle" has been on my mind a lot. I have often thought that He has overestimated my ability! Like most people, I sometimes feel stuck and unable to clearly see the direction I should maneuver my life. One thing I do know is that staying in place will continue that feeling of being stuck. Only through movement will life continue to flourish. I came across a quote from this very wise man:

If you are going through hell, keep going.
— Winston Churchill

At times, life can be challenging, miserable, and traumatic. If we keep going though, we are sure to see the rainbow, smiles, and joy. The key to life is to not stay stuck, but rather to keep moving. Sure, it may take all your effort to get up and do what needs to be done, but go ahead! Sometimes the simple task of mundane housework is enough to spark a change. Other times, you need to challenge yourself in a much larger way. You may have to get out of bed, when all you want to do is cry under the covers, or you may have to face the person who has just knocked away your confidence. It is finding your inner strength. No one ever promised you that life would be easy. But you are worth the effort. Your path may take you through hell, but keep going and the scenery will change!

May you keep moving forward through every challenge!

Focus

Recall a time you have "gone through hell" (or maybe you're currently experiencing this). On the next few pages, document what you did to keep yourself moving forward, or challenge yourself on what you need to do currently. Then if you need to be reminded in the future, you have a road map to get you through any challenging times.